GOAL PLANNER

This book belongs to:

NAME:

CONTACT:

DAILY GOAL
PLANNER

THE GOAL

START:

FINISH:

IHEAS \ SKETCHES

PURCHASE

THE CHALLACE

ACTIONS STEPS

1.
2.
3.
4.
5.
6.
7.

NOTES

YOUR CELEBRATION

DAILY GOAL
PLANNER

THE GOAL

START:

FINISH:

IHEAS \ SKETCHES

PURCHASE

THE CHALLACE

ACTIONS STEPS

1.
2.
3.
4.
5.
6.
7.

NOTES

YOUR CELEBRATION

DAILY GOAL
PLANNER

THE GOAL

START:

FINISH:

IHEAS \ SKETCHES

PURCHASE

THE CHALLACE

ACTIONS STEPS

1.
2.
3.
4.
5.
6.
7.

NOTES

YOUR CELEBRATION

DAILY GOAL
PLANNER

THE GOAL

START:

FINISH:

IHEAS \ SKETCHES

PURCHASE

THE CHALLACE

ACTIONS STEPS

1.
2.
3.
4.
5.
6.
7.

NOTES

YOUR CELEBRATION

DAILY GOAL
PLANNER

THE GOAL

START:

FINISH:

IHEAS \ SKETCHES

PURCHASE

THE CHALLACE

ACTIONS STEPS

1.
2.
3.
4.
5.
6.
7.

NOTES

YOUR CELEBRATION

DAILY GOAL
PLANNER

THE GOAL

START:

FINISH:

IHEAS \ SKETCHES

PURCHASE

THE CHALLACE

ACTIONS STEPS

1.
2.
3.
4.
5.
6.
7.

NOTES

YOUR CELEBRATION

DAILY GOAL
PLANNER

THE GOAL

START:

FINISH:

IHEAS \ SKETCHES

PURCHASE

THE CHALLACE

ACTIONS STEPS

1.
2.
3.
4.
5.
6.
7.

NOTES

YOUR CELEBRATION

DAILY GOAL
PLANNER

THE GOAL

START:

FINISH:

IHEAS \ SKETCHES

PURCHASE

THE CHALLACE

ACTIONS STEPS

1.
2.
3.
4.
5.
6.
7.

NOTES

YOUR CELEBRATION

DAILY GOAL
PLANNER

THE GOAL

START:

FINISH:

IHEAS \ SKETCHES

PURCHASE

THE CHALLACE

ACTIONS STEPS

1.
2.
3.
4.
5.
6.
7.

NOTES

YOUR CELEBRATION

DAILY GOAL
PLANNER

THE GOAL

START:

FINISH:

IHEAS \ SKETCHES

PURCHASE

THE CHALLACE

ACTIONS STEPS

1.
2.
3.
4.
5.
6.
7.

NOTES

YOUR CELEBRATION

DAILY GOAL
PLANNER

THE GOAL

START:

FINISH:

IHEAS \ SKETCHES

PURCHASE

THE CHALLACE

ACTIONS STEPS

1.
2.
3.
4.
5.
6.
7.

NOTES

YOUR CELEBRATION

DAILY GOAL
PLANNER

THE GOAL

START:

FINISH:

IHEAS \ SKETCHES

PURCHASE

THE CHALLACE

ACTIONS STEPS

1.
2.
3.
4.
5.
6.
7.

NOTES

YOUR CELEBRATION

DAILY GOAL
PLANNER

THE GOAL

START:

FINISH:

IHEAS \ SKETCHES

PURCHASE

THE CHALLACE

ACTIONS STEPS

1.
2.
3.
4.
5.
6.
7.

NOTES

YOUR CELEBRATION

DAILY GOAL
PLANNER

THE GOAL

START:

FINISH:

IHEAS \ SKETCHES

PURCHASE

THE CHALLACE

ACTIONS STEPS

1.
2.
3.
4.
5.
6.
7.

NOTES

YOUR CELEBRATION

DAILY GOAL
PLANNER

THE GOAL	
	START:
	FINISH:

IHEAS \ SKETCHES

PURCHASE

THE CHALLACE

ACTIONS STEPS

1.
2.
3.
4.
5.
6.
7.

NOTES

YOUR CELEBRATION

DAILY GOAL
PLANNER

THE GOAL

START:

FINISH:

IHEAS \ SKETCHES

PURCHASE

THE CHALLACE

ACTIONS STEPS

1.
2.
3.
4.
5.
6.
7.

NOTES

YOUR CELEBRATION

DAILY GOAL
PLANNER

THE GOAL

START:

FINISH:

IHEAS \ SKETCHES

PURCHASE

THE CHALLACE

ACTIONS STEPS

1.
2.
3.
4.
5.
6.
7.

NOTES

YOUR CELEBRATION

DAILY GOAL
PLANNER

THE GOAL

START:

FINISH:

IHEAS \ SKETCHES

PURCHASE

THE CHALLACE

ACTIONS STEPS

1.
2.
3.
4.
5.
6.
7.

NOTES

YOUR CELEBRATION

DAILY GOAL
PLANNER

THE GOAL

START:

FINISH:

IHEAS \ SKETCHES

PURCHASE

THE CHALLACE

ACTIONS STEPS

1.
2.
3.
4.
5.
6.
7.

NOTES

YOUR CELEBRATION

DAILY GOAL
PLANNER

THE GOAL

START:

FINISH:

IHEAS \ SKETCHES

PURCHASE

THE CHALLACE

ACTIONS STEPS

1.
2.
3.
4.
5.
6.
7.

NOTES

YOUR CELEBRATION

DAILY GOAL
PLANNER

THE GOAL

START:

FINISH:

IHEAS \ SKETCHES

PURCHASE

THE CHALLACE

ACTIONS STEPS

1.
2.
3.
4.
5.
6.
7.

NOTES

YOUR CELEBRATION

DAILY GOAL
PLANNER

THE GOAL

START:

FINISH:

IHEAS \ SKETCHES

PURCHASE

THE CHALLACE

ACTIONS STEPS

1.
2.
3.
4.
5.
6.
7.

NOTES

YOUR CELEBRATION

DAILY GOAL
PLANNER

THE GOAL

START:

FINISH:

IHEAS \ SKETCHES

PURCHASE

THE CHALLACE

ACTIONS STEPS

1.
2.
3.
4.
5.
6.
7.

NOTES

YOUR CELEBRATION

DAILY GOAL
PLANNER

THE GOAL

START:

FINISH:

IHEAS \ SKETCHES

PURCHASE

THE CHALLACE

ACTIONS STEPS

1.
2.
3.
4.
5.
6.
7.

NOTES

YOUR CELEBRATION

DAILY GOAL
PLANNER

THE GOAL

START:

FINISH:

IHEAS \ SKETCHES

PURCHASE

THE CHALLACE

ACTIONS STEPS

1.
2.
3.
4.
5.
6.
7.

NOTES

YOUR CELEBRATION

DAILY GOAL
PLANNER

THE GOAL

START:

FINISH:

IHEAS \ SKETCHES

PURCHASE

THE CHALLACE

ACTIONS STEPS

1.
2.
3.
4.
5.
6.
7.

NOTES

YOUR CELEBRATION

DAILY GOAL
PLANNER

THE GOAL

START:

FINISH:

IHEAS \ SKETCHES

PURCHASE

THE CHALLACE

ACTIONS STEPS

1.
2.
3.
4.
5.
6.
7.

NOTES

YOUR CELEBRATION

DAILY GOAL
PLANNER

THE GOAL

START:

FINISH:

IHEAS \ SKETCHES

PURCHASE

THE CHALLACE

ACTIONS STEPS

1.
2.
3.
4.
5.
6.
7.

NOTES

YOUR CELEBRATION

DAILY GOAL
PLANNER

THE GOAL

START:

FINISH:

IHEAS \ SKETCHES

PURCHASE

THE CHALLACE

ACTIONS STEPS

1.
2.
3.
4.
5.
6.
7.

NOTES

YOUR CELEBRATION

DAILY GOAL
PLANNER

THE GOAL

START:

FINISH:

IHEAS \ SKETCHES

PURCHASE

THE CHALLACE

ACTIONS STEPS

1.
2.
3.
4.
5.
6.
7.

NOTES

YOUR CELEBRATION

DAILY GOAL
PLANNER

THE GOAL

START:

FINISH:

IHEAS \ SKETCHES

PURCHASE

THE CHALLACE

ACTIONS STEPS

1.
2.
3.
4.
5.
6.
7.

NOTES

YOUR CELEBRATION

DAILY GOAL
PLANNER

THE GOAL

START:

FINISH:

IHEAS \ SKETCHES

PURCHASE

THE CHALLACE

ACTIONS STEPS

1.
2.
3.
4.
5.
6.
7.

NOTES

YOUR CELEBRATION

DAILY GOAL
PLANNER

THE GOAL

START:

FINISH:

IHEAS \ SKETCHES

PURCHASE

THE CHALLACE

ACTIONS STEPS

1.
2.
3.
4.
5.
6.
7.

NOTES

YOUR CELEBRATION

DAILY GOAL
PLANNER

THE GOAL

START:

FINISH:

IHEAS \ SKETCHES

PURCHASE

THE CHALLACE

ACTIONS STEPS

1.
2.
3.
4.
5.
6.
7.

NOTES

YOUR CELEBRATION

DAILY GOAL
PLANNER

THE GOAL

START:

FINISH:

IHEAS \ SKETCHES

PURCHASE

THE CHALLACE

ACTIONS STEPS

1.
2.
3.
4.
5.
6.
7.

NOTES

YOUR CELEBRATION

DAILY GOAL
PLANNER

THE GOAL

START:

FINISH:

IHEAS \ SKETCHES

PURCHASE

THE CHALLACE

ACTIONS STEPS

1.
2.
3.
4.
5.
6.
7.

NOTES

YOUR CELEBRATION

DAILY GOAL
PLANNER

THE GOAL

START:

FINISH:

IHEAS \ SKETCHES

PURCHASE

THE CHALLACE

ACTIONS STEPS

1.
2.
3.
4.
5.
6.
7.

NOTES

YOUR CELEBRATION

DAILY GOAL
PLANNER

THE GOAL

START:

FINISH:

IHEAS \ SKETCHES

PURCHASE

THE CHALLACE

ACTIONS STEPS

1.
2.
3.
4.
5.
6.
7.

NOTES

YOUR CELEBRATION

DAILY GOAL
PLANNER

THE GOAL

START:

FINISH:

IHEAS \ SKETCHES

PURCHASE

THE CHALLACE

ACTIONS STEPS

1.
2.
3.
4.
5.
6.
7.

NOTES

YOUR CELEBRATION

DAILY GOAL
PLANNER

THE GOAL

START:

FINISH:

IHEAS \ SKETCHES

PURCHASE

THE CHALLACE

ACTIONS STEPS

1.
2.
3.
4.
5.
6.
7.

NOTES

YOUR CELEBRATION

DAILY GOAL
PLANNER

THE GOAL

START:

FINISH:

IHEAS \ SKETCHES

PURCHASE

THE CHALLACE

ACTIONS STEPS

1.
2.
3.
4.
5.
6.
7.

NOTES

YOUR CELEBRATION

DAILY GOAL
PLANNER

THE GOAL

START:

FINISH:

IHEAS \ SKETCHES

PURCHASE

THE CHALLACE

ACTIONS STEPS

1.
2.
3.
4.
5.
6.
7.

NOTES

YOUR CELEBRATION

DAILY GOAL
PLANNER

THE GOAL

START:

FINISH:

IHEAS \ SKETCHES

PURCHASE

THE CHALLACE

ACTIONS STEPS

1.
2.
3.
4.
5.
6.
7.

NOTES

YOUR CELEBRATION

DAILY GOAL
PLANNER

THE GOAL

START:

FINISH:

IHEAS \ SKETCHES

PURCHASE

THE CHALLACE

ACTIONS STEPS

1.
2.
3.
4.
5.
6.
7.

NOTES

YOUR CELEBRATION

DAILY GOAL
PLANNER

THE GOAL

START:

FINISH:

IHEAS \ SKETCHES

PURCHASE

THE CHALLACE

ACTIONS STEPS

1.
2.
3.
4.
5.
6.
7.

NOTES

YOUR CELEBRATION

DAILY GOAL
PLANNER

THE GOAL

START:

FINISH:

IHEAS \ SKETCHES

PURCHASE

THE CHALLACE

ACTIONS STEPS

1.
2.
3.
4.
5.
6.
7.

NOTES

YOUR CELEBRATION

DAILY GOAL
PLANNER

THE GOAL

START:

FINISH:

IHEAS \ SKETCHES

PURCHASE

THE CHALLACE

ACTIONS STEPS

1.
2.
3.
4.
5.
6.
7.

NOTES

YOUR CELEBRATION

DAILY GOAL
PLANNER

THE GOAL

START:

FINISH:

IHEAS \ SKETCHES

PURCHASE

THE CHALLACE

ACTIONS STEPS

1.
2.
3.
4.
5.
6.
7.

NOTES

YOUR CELEBRATION

DAILY GOAL
PLANNER

THE GOAL

START:

FINISH:

IHEAS \ SKETCHES

PURCHASE

THE CHALLACE

ACTIONS STEPS

1.
2.
3.
4.
5.
6.
7.

NOTES

YOUR CELEBRATION

DAILY GOAL
PLANNER

THE GOAL

START:

FINISH:

IHEAS \ SKETCHES

PURCHASE

THE CHALLACE

ACTIONS STEPS

1.
2.
3.
4.
5.
6.
7.

NOTES

YOUR CELEBRATION

DAILY GOAL
PLANNER

THE GOAL

START:

FINISH:

IHEAS \ SKETCHES

PURCHASE

THE CHALLACE

ACTIONS STEPS

1.
2.
3.
4.
5.
6.
7.

NOTES

YOUR CELEBRATION

DAILY GOAL
PLANNER

THE GOAL

START:

FINISH:

IHEAS \ SKETCHES

PURCHASE

THE CHALLACE

ACTIONS STEPS

1.
2.
3.
4.
5.
6.
7.

NOTES

YOUR CELEBRATION

DAILY GOAL
PLANNER

THE GOAL	
	START:
	FINISH:

IHEAS \ SKETCHES

PURCHASE

THE CHALLACE

ACTIONS STEPS

1.
2.
3.
4.
5.
6.
7.

NOTES

YOUR CELEBRATION

DAILY GOAL
PLANNER

THE GOAL

START:

FINISH:

IHEAS \ SKETCHES

PURCHASE

THE CHALLACE

ACTIONS STEPS

1.
2.
3.
4.
5.
6.
7.

NOTES

YOUR CELEBRATION

DAILY GOAL
PLANNER

THE GOAL

START:

FINISH:

IHEAS \ SKETCHES

PURCHASE

THE CHALLACE

ACTIONS STEPS

1.
2.
3.
4.
5.
6.
7.

NOTES

YOUR CELEBRATION

DAILY GOAL
PLANNER

THE GOAL

START:

FINISH:

IHEAS \ SKETCHES

PURCHASE

THE CHALLACE

ACTIONS STEPS

1.
2.
3.
4.
5.
6.
7.

NOTES

YOUR CELEBRATION

DAILY GOAL
PLANNER

THE GOAL

START:

FINISH:

IHEAS \ SKETCHES

PURCHASE

THE CHALLACE

ACTIONS STEPS

1.
2.
3.
4.
5.
6.
7.

NOTES

YOUR CELEBRATION

DAILY GOAL
PLANNER

THE GOAL

START:

FINISH:

IHEAS \ SKETCHES

PURCHASE

THE CHALLACE

ACTIONS STEPS

1.
2.
3.
4.
5.
6.
7.

NOTES

YOUR CELEBRATION

DAILY GOAL
PLANNER

THE GOAL

START:

FINISH:

IHEAS \ SKETCHES

PURCHASE

THE CHALLACE

ACTIONS STEPS

1.
2.
3.
4.
5.
6.
7.

NOTES

YOUR CELEBRATION

DAILY GOAL
PLANNER

THE GOAL

START:

FINISH:

IHEAS \ SKETCHES

PURCHASE

THE CHALLACE

ACTIONS STEPS

1.
2.
3.
4.
5.
6.
7.

NOTES

YOUR CELEBRATION

DAILY GOAL
PLANNER

THE GOAL

START:

FINISH:

IHEAS \ SKETCHES

PURCHASE

THE CHALLACE

ACTIONS STEPS

1.
2.
3.
4.
5.
6.
7.

NOTES

YOUR CELEBRATION

DAILY GOAL
PLANNER

THE GOAL

START:

FINISH:

IHEAS \ SKETCHES

PURCHASE

THE CHALLACE

ACTIONS STEPS

1.
2.
3.
4.
5.
6.
7.

NOTES

YOUR CELEBRATION

DAILY GOAL
PLANNER

THE GOAL

START:

FINISH:

IHEAS \ SKETCHES

PURCHASE

THE CHALLACE

ACTIONS STEPS

1.
2.
3.
4.
5.
6.
7.

NOTES

YOUR CELEBRATION

DAILY GOAL
PLANNER

THE GOAL

START:

FINISH:

IHEAS \ SKETCHES

PURCHASE

THE CHALLACE

ACTIONS STEPS

1.
2.
3.
4.
5.
6.
7.

NOTES

YOUR CELEBRATION

DAILY GOAL
PLANNER

THE GOAL

START:

FINISH:

IHEAS \ SKETCHES

PURCHASE

THE CHALLACE

ACTIONS STEPS

1.
2.
3.
4.
5.
6.
7.

NOTES

YOUR CELEBRATION

DAILY GOAL
PLANNER

THE GOAL

START:

FINISH:

IHEAS \ SKETCHES

PURCHASE

THE CHALLACE

ACTIONS STEPS

1.
2.
3.
4.
5.
6.
7.

NOTES

YOUR CELEBRATION

DAILY GOAL
PLANNER

THE GOAL

START:

FINISH:

IHEAS \ SKETCHES

PURCHASE

THE CHALLACE

ACTIONS STEPS

1.
2.
3.
4.
5.
6.
7.

NOTES

YOUR CELEBRATION

DAILY GOAL
PLANNER

THE GOAL

START:

FINISH:

IHEAS \ SKETCHES

PURCHASE

THE CHALLACE

ACTIONS STEPS

1.
2.
3.
4.
5.
6.
7.

NOTES

YOUR CELEBRATION

DAILY GOAL
PLANNER

THE GOAL

START:

FINISH:

IHEAS \ SKETCHES

PURCHASE

THE CHALLACE

ACTIONS STEPS

1.
2.
3.
4.
5.
6.
7.

NOTES

YOUR CELEBRATION

DAILY GOAL
PLANNER

THE GOAL

START:

FINISH:

IHEAS \ SKETCHES

PURCHASE

THE CHALLACE

ACTIONS STEPS

1.
2.
3.
4.
5.
6.
7.

NOTES

YOUR CELEBRATION

DAILY GOAL
PLANNER

THE GOAL

START:

FINISH:

IHEAS \ SKETCHES

PURCHASE

THE CHALLACE

ACTIONS STEPS

1.
2.
3.
4.
5.
6.
7.

NOTES

YOUR CELEBRATION

DAILY GOAL
PLANNER

THE GOAL

START:

FINISH:

IHEAS \ SKETCHES

PURCHASE

THE CHALLACE

ACTIONS STEPS

1.
2.
3.
4.
5.
6.
7.

NOTES

YOUR CELEBRATION

DAILY GOAL
PLANNER

THE GOAL

START:

FINISH:

IHEAS \ SKETCHES

PURCHASE

THE CHALLACE

ACTIONS STEPS

1.
2.
3.
4.
5.
6.
7.

NOTES

YOUR CELEBRATION

DAILY GOAL
PLANNER

THE GOAL

START:

FINISH:

IHEAS \ SKETCHES

PURCHASE

THE CHALLACE

ACTIONS STEPS

1.
2.
3.
4.
5.
6.
7.

NOTES

YOUR CELEBRATION

DAILY GOAL
PLANNER

THE GOAL

START:

FINISH:

IHEAS \ SKETCHES

PURCHASE

THE CHALLACE

ACTIONS STEPS

1.
2.
3.
4.
5.
6.
7.

NOTES

YOUR CELEBRATION

DAILY GOAL
PLANNER

THE GOAL

START:

FINISH:

IHEAS \ SKETCHES

PURCHASE

THE CHALLACE

ACTIONS STEPS

1.
2.
3.
4.
5.
6.
7.

NOTES

YOUR CELEBRATION

DAILY GOAL
PLANNER

THE GOAL

START:

FINISH:

IHEAS \ SKETCHES

PURCHASE

THE CHALLACE

ACTIONS STEPS

1.
2.
3.
4.
5.
6.
7.

NOTES

YOUR CELEBRATION

DAILY GOAL
PLANNER

THE GOAL

START:

FINISH:

IHEAS \ SKETCHES

PURCHASE

THE CHALLACE

ACTIONS STEPS

1.
2.
3.
4.
5.
6.
7.

NOTES

YOUR CELEBRATION

DAILY GOAL
PLANNER

THE GOAL

START:

FINISH:

IHEAS \ SKETCHES

PURCHASE

THE CHALLACE

ACTIONS STEPS

1.
2.
3.
4.
5.
6.
7.

NOTES

YOUR CELEBRATION

DAILY GOAL
PLANNER

THE GOAL

START:

FINISH:

IHEAS \ SKETCHES

PURCHASE

THE CHALLACE

ACTIONS STEPS

1.
2.
3.
4.
5.
6.
7.

NOTES

YOUR CELEBRATION

DAILY GOAL
PLANNER

THE GOAL

START:

FINISH:

IHEAS \ SKETCHES

PURCHASE

THE CHALLACE

ACTIONS STEPS

1.
2.
3.
4.
5.
6.
7.

NOTES

YOUR CELEBRATION

DAILY GOAL
PLANNER

THE GOAL

START:

FINISH:

IHEAS \ SKETCHES

PURCHASE

THE CHALLACE

ACTIONS STEPS

1.
2.
3.
4.
5.
6.
7.

NOTES

YOUR CELEBRATION

DAILY GOAL
PLANNER

THE GOAL

START:

FINISH:

IHEAS \ SKETCHES

PURCHASE

THE CHALLACE

ACTIONS STEPS

1.
2.
3.
4.
5.
6.
7.

NOTES

YOUR CELEBRATION

DAILY GOAL
PLANNER

THE GOAL

START:

FINISH:

IHEAS \ SKETCHES

PURCHASE

THE CHALLACE

ACTIONS STEPS

1.
2.
3.
4.
5.
6.
7.

NOTES

YOUR CELEBRATION

DAILY GOAL
PLANNER

THE GOAL

START:

FINISH:

IHEAS \ SKETCHES

PURCHASE

THE CHALLACE

ACTIONS STEPS

1.
2.
3.
4.
5.
6.
7.

NOTES

YOUR CELEBRATION

DAILY GOAL
PLANNER

THE GOAL

START:

FINISH:

IHEAS \ SKETCHES

PURCHASE

THE CHALLACE

ACTIONS STEPS

1.
2.
3.
4.
5.
6.
7.

NOTES

YOUR CELEBRATION

DAILY GOAL
PLANNER

THE GOAL

START:

FINISH:

IHEAS \ SKETCHES

PURCHASE

THE CHALLACE

ACTIONS STEPS

1.
2.
3.
4.
5.
6.
7.

NOTES

YOUR CELEBRATION

DAILY GOAL
PLANNER

THE GOAL

START:

FINISH:

IHEAS \ SKETCHES

PURCHASE

THE CHALLACE

ACTIONS STEPS

1.
2.
3.
4.
5.
6.
7.

NOTES

YOUR CELEBRATION

DAILY GOAL
PLANNER

THE GOAL

START:

FINISH:

IHEAS \ SKETCHES

PURCHASE

THE CHALLACE

ACTIONS STEPS

1.
2.
3.
4.
5.
6.
7.

NOTES

YOUR CELEBRATION

DAILY GOAL
PLANNER

THE GOAL

START:

FINISH:

IHEAS \ SKETCHES

PURCHASE

THE CHALLACE

ACTIONS STEPS

1.
2.
3.
4.
5.
6.
7.

NOTES

YOUR CELEBRATION

DAILY GOAL
PLANNER

THE GOAL

START:

FINISH:

IHEAS \ SKETCHES

PURCHASE

THE CHALLACE

ACTIONS STEPS

1.
2.
3.
4.
5.
6.
7.

NOTES

YOUR CELEBRATION

DAILY GOAL
PLANNER

THE GOAL

START:

FINISH:

IHEAS \ SKETCHES

PURCHASE

THE CHALLACE

ACTIONS STEPS

1.
2.
3.
4.
5.
6.
7.

NOTES

YOUR CELEBRATION

DAILY GOAL
PLANNER

THE GOAL

START:

FINISH:

IHEAS \ SKETCHES

PURCHASE

THE CHALLACE

ACTIONS STEPS

1.
2.
3.
4.
5.
6.
7.

NOTES

YOUR CELEBRATION

DAILY GOAL
PLANNER

THE GOAL

START:

FINISH:

IHEAS \ SKETCHES

PURCHASE

THE CHALLACE

ACTIONS STEPS

1.
2.
3.
4.
5.
6.
7.

NOTES

YOUR CELEBRATION

DAILY GOAL
PLANNER

THE GOAL

START:

FINISH:

IHEAS \ SKETCHES

PURCHASE

THE CHALLACE

ACTIONS STEPS

1.
2.
3.
4.
5.
6.
7.

NOTES

YOUR CELEBRATION

DAILY GOAL
PLANNER

THE GOAL

START:

FINISH:

IHEAS \ SKETCHES

PURCHASE

THE CHALLACE

ACTIONS STEPS

1.
2.
3.
4.
5.
6.
7.

NOTES

YOUR CELEBRATION

DAILY GOAL
PLANNER

THE GOAL

START:

FINISH:

IHEAS \ SKETCHES

PURCHASE

THE CHALLACE

ACTIONS STEPS

1.
2.
3.
4.
5.
6.
7.

NOTES

YOUR CELEBRATION

DAILY GOAL
PLANNER

THE GOAL

START:

FINISH:

IHEAS \ SKETCHES

PURCHASE

THE CHALLACE

ACTIONS STEPS

1.
2.
3.
4.
5.
6.
7.

NOTES

YOUR CELEBRATION

DAILY GOAL
PLANNER

THE GOAL

START:

FINISH:

IHEAS \ SKETCHES

PURCHASE

THE CHALLACE

ACTIONS STEPS

1.
2.
3.
4.
5.
6.
7.

NOTES

YOUR CELEBRATION

DAILY GOAL
PLANNER

THE GOAL

START:

FINISH:

IHEAS \ SKETCHES

PURCHASE

THE CHALLACE

ACTIONS STEPS

1.
2.
3.
4.
5.
6.
7.

NOTES

YOUR CELEBRATION

DAILY GOAL
PLANNER

THE GOAL

START:

FINISH:

IHEAS \ SKETCHES

PURCHASE

THE CHALLACE

ACTIONS STEPS

1.
2.
3.
4.
5.
6.
7.

NOTES

YOUR CELEBRATION

DAILY GOAL
PLANNER

THE GOAL

START:

FINISH:

IHEAS \ SKETCHES

PURCHASE

THE CHALLACE

ACTIONS STEPS

NOTES

1.
2.
3.
4.
5.
6.
7.

YOUR CELEBRATION

DAILY GOAL
PLANNER

THE GOAL

START:

FINISH:

IHEAS \ SKETCHES

PURCHASE

THE CHALLACE

ACTIONS STEPS

1.
2.
3.
4.
5.
6.
7.

NOTES

YOUR CELEBRATION

DAILY GOAL
PLANNER

THE GOAL

START:

FINISH:

IHEAS \ SKETCHES

PURCHASE

THE CHALLACE

ACTIONS STEPS

1.
2.
3.
4.
5.
6.
7.

NOTES

YOUR CELEBRATION

DAILY GOAL
PLANNER

THE GOAL

START:

FINISH:

IHEAS \ SKETCHES

PURCHASE

THE CHALLACE

ACTIONS STEPS

1.
2.
3.
4.
5.
6.
7.

NOTES

YOUR CELEBRATION

DAILY GOAL
PLANNER

THE GOAL

START:

FINISH:

IHEAS \ SKETCHES

PURCHASE

THE CHALLACE

ACTIONS STEPS

1.
2.
3.
4.
5.
6.
7.

NOTES

YOUR CELEBRATION

DAILY GOAL
PLANNER

THE GOAL

START:

FINISH:

IHEAS \ SKETCHES

PURCHASE

THE CHALLACE

ACTIONS STEPS

1.
2.
3.
4.
5.
6.
7.

NOTES

YOUR CELEBRATION

DAILY GOAL
PLANNER

THE GOAL

START:

FINISH:

IHEAS \ SKETCHES

PURCHASE

THE CHALLACE

ACTIONS STEPS

1.
2.
3.
4.
5.
6.
7.

NOTES

YOUR CELEBRATION

DAILY GOAL
PLANNER

THE GOAL

START:

FINISH:

IHEAS \ SKETCHES

PURCHASE

THE CHALLACE

ACTIONS STEPS

1.
2.
3.
4.
5.
6.
7.

NOTES

YOUR CELEBRATION

DAILY GOAL
PLANNER

THE GOAL

START:

FINISH:

IHEAS \ SKETCHES

PURCHASE

THE CHALLACE

ACTIONS STEPS

1.
2.
3.
4.
5.
6.
7.

NOTES

YOUR CELEBRATION

DAILY GOAL
PLANNER

THE GOAL

START:

FINISH:

IHEAS \ SKETCHES

PURCHASE

THE CHALLACE

ACTIONS STEPS

1.
2.
3.
4.
5.
6.
7.

NOTES

YOUR CELEBRATION

DAILY GOAL
PLANNER

THE GOAL

START:

FINISH:

IHEAS \ SKETCHES

PURCHASE

THE CHALLACE

ACTIONS STEPS

1.
2.
3.
4.
5.
6.
7.

NOTES

YOUR CELEBRATION

DAILY GOAL
PLANNER

THE GOAL

START:

FINISH:

IHEAS \ SKETCHES

PURCHASE

THE CHALLACE

ACTIONS STEPS

1.
2.
3.
4.
5.
6.
7.

NOTES

YOUR CELEBRATION

DAILY GOAL
PLANNER

THE GOAL

START:

FINISH:

IHEAS \ SKETCHES

PURCHASE

THE CHALLACE

ACTIONS STEPS

1.
2.
3.
4.
5.
6.
7.

NOTES

YOUR CELEBRATION

DAILY GOAL
PLANNER

THE GOAL

START:

FINISH:

IHEAS \ SKETCHES

PURCHASE

THE CHALLACE

ACTIONS STEPS

1.
2.
3.
4.
5.
6.
7.

NOTES

YOUR CELEBRATION

DAILY GOAL
PLANNER

THE GOAL

START:

FINISH:

IHEAS \ SKETCHES

PURCHASE

THE CHALLACE

ACTIONS STEPS

1.
2.
3.
4.
5.
6.
7.

NOTES

YOUR CELEBRATION

DAILY GOAL
PLANNER

THE GOAL

START:

FINISH:

IHEAS \ SKETCHES

PURCHASE

THE CHALLACE

ACTIONS STEPS

1.
2.
3.
4.
5.
6.
7.

NOTES

YOUR CELEBRATION

DAILY GOAL
PLANNER

THE GOAL

START:

FINISH:

IHEAS \ SKETCHES

PURCHASE

THE CHALLACE

ACTIONS STEPS

1.
2.
3.
4.
5.
6.
7.

NOTES

YOUR CELEBRATION

DAILY GOAL
PLANNER

THE GOAL

START:

FINISH:

IHEAS \ SKETCHES

PURCHASE

THE CHALLACE

ACTIONS STEPS

1.
2.
3.
4.
5.
6.
7.

NOTES

YOUR CELEBRATION